D1135582

COOKING FOR YOUR CAT

HEALTHY RECIPES – SEASONED WITH AFFECTION

Sophie Klein

PaRragon

Bath · New York · Singapore · Hong Kong · Cologne · Delhi
Melbourne · Amsterdam · Johannesburg · Auckland · Shenzhen

All the recipes in this book have been carefully researched and formulated, and have been tried out on various cats. However, we cannot rule out the possibility of particular food intolerances in certain cats. The publisher and the author cannot be held liable in this case.

The recipes are intended for special occasions; in other words, they are meant to be used as an addition to your cat's regular diet. They cannot and should not replace a proper balanced diet. If you are uncertain about your cat's tolerance of an ingredient or preparation method, please consult your vet. With very young cats, pregnant cats, cats that are ill and cats that have to keep to a particular diet, it is essential to ask the advice of your vet before feeding them home-made food.

Not everything that humans like to eat is good for cats. Alcohol, cocoa, chocolate, raw pork (including raw bacon and salami), avocado, onions, garlic, strong spices, sugar and excessive salt are all known to be harmful. This list does not claim to be comprehensive.

Written by Sophie Klein
Illustrated by Kyra Stempell

This edition published by Parragon in 2011

Copyright © Parragon Books Ltd 2009
Queen Street House, 4 Queen Street, Bath BA1 1HE, UK

All rights reserved. No part of this publication may be reproduced, stored in a retrieval system or transmitted, in any form or by any means, electronic, mechanical, photocopying, recording or otherwise, without the prior permission of the copyright holder.

ISBN: 978-1-4454-1594-9

Printed in China

Original German edition created and produced by
Production: ditter.projektagentur GmbH; Project coordination: Michael Ditter; Photographer: Jo Kirchherr; Home Economist: Sonja Schubert; Illustrations: Kyra Stempell; Editing: Sebnem Yavuz; Design: Sabine Vonderstein; Lithography: Klaussner Medien Service GmbH

English-language edition produced by
Cambridge Publishing Management Ltd
Translator: Jackie Smith

The publisher wishes to express particular thanks to Dr. Burton Miller, renowned holistic doctor of veterinary medicine, for his careful advice on the recipes included in this book. Based in Huntington, NY, Dr. Miller is the founder of the Animal Wellness Center (www.animalwellness.net).

This book uses both metric and imperial measurements. Follow the same units of measurement throughout; do not mix metric and imperial. All spoon measurements are level: teaspoons are assumed to be 5 ml, and tablespoons are assumed to be 15 ml. Unless otherwise stated, milk is assumed to be full fat, and eggs and individual vegetables are medium, and pepper is freshly ground black pepper.

The times given are an approximate guide only. Preparation times differ according to the techniques used by different people and the cooking times may also vary from those given. Optional ingredients, variations or serving suggestions have not been included in the calculations.

Contents

Foreword

Cats are connoisseurs. Unlike dogs, they tend to be very fussy and whimsical, not just about their food. If their normal feeding routines are disturbed or their menu changes dramatically, they soon become moody and reject unfamiliar food. Cats are also curious, though; if you leave them in peace and give them time, they will eventually embark on a cautious investigation of the contents of their food bowl before enjoying the tasty new morsels you have served.

My cat always used to rub affectionately around my legs when I was preparing all kinds of tasty dishes for myself and my guests. It was this that caused me to set aside a small portion of the ingredients during preparation, so that I could cook up a cat's dinner in a separate pan for my four-legged friend. For example, 'Lucca's favourite risotto' was derived from an asparagus risotto with grilled chicken breast cooked for human consumption, while the minced meat for our own meatballs was transformed, with the addition of some cheese, porridge oats and egg, into 'Lady's cheese balls'.

After a while I had assembled a whole collection of recipes for little dishes for cats – which is what formed the basis for this cookbook. The dishes are easy to prepare, and have been tested on many occasions by my cat Paula and her friends. However, the recipes are meant as gourmet treats for special occasions, and are not intended to take the place of a cat's regular daily diet. I serve up these dishes twice a week at most, to supplement my cat's diet or as a reward. If you want to feed your cat only home-made food, it is important to seek the advice of a vet beforehand, and to find out about the essential components of a healthy feline diet. My recipes are not suitable for cats that are ill or that have to follow a particular diet.

When cooking for healthy cats, there are still certain rules that must be adhered to. Not everything that humans like to eat is good for cats. Alcohol, cocoa, chocolate, raw pork (including raw bacon and salami), avocado, onions, garlic, strong spices, sugar and excessive salt are definitely known to be harmful. Rice, potatoes, pasta, fish and poultry must only be given cooked, and no bones (meat or fish) should ever be put in a cat's bowl. Please soak cereal flakes and grains to soften them before feeding to your cat, and finely chop or grate vegetables. Artificial colourings and flavourings must be avoided.

If, despite all the loving care you put into cooking it, your cat leaves its meal untouched, do not be disappointed, and whatever happens do not let your furry friend go hungry as a punishment. Just try again another day with a different recipe. Every cat has its own preferences. My Paula feasted on the fish dishes, and the fish munchies and chicken chips, with particular enthusiasm. The many other grateful taste-testers also voiced their approval with contented purring. Paula and I would like to take this opportunity to thank them and their owners once again.

Sophie Klein

FOR SOUP LOVERS

CLASSIC CHICKEN SOUP

Makes 2 to 3 portions

For the chicken stock:
1 litre (1¾ pints) water
¼ tsp salt
2 skinless chicken thighs
2 carrots, peeled and diced
100 g (3½ oz) celery stick, washed
  and diced

For the soup:
20 g (¾ oz) carrot, grated
1 tsp vegetable oil
10 g (¼ oz) cooked rice
½ tsp freshly chopped flat-leaf parsley

For the chicken stock, bring the water to a boil in a saucepan with the salt, and add the chicken thighs and the vegetables. Simmer, covered, for 45 minutes, remove from the heat and allow to cool.

Remove the chicken thighs from the stock and take the meat off the bones. Discard the bones. Strain the stock into a bowl and discard the vegetables. Measure out 100 ml (3½ fl oz) stock and 100 g (3½ oz) chicken for the chicken soup, and put to one side. The remaining stock and chicken can be used for other dishes or frozen.

For the soup, peel and grate the carrot. Heat the oil in a saucepan, and sauté the rice and grated carrot. Pour in the measured quantity of stock, bring to the boil and simmer for 10 minutes.

Meanwhile, finely chop the weighed-out chicken. Remove the soup from the heat. Add the chicken and parsley, and allow to cool to room temperature. Serve a portion at a time.

FISH SOUP FOR CHICO

Makes 2 to 3 portions

40 g (1½ oz) salmon fillet, skinless and boneless
40 g (1½ oz) mackerel fillet, skinless and boneless
20 g (¾ oz) raw prawns, peeled
20 g (¾ oz) courgette
1 tsp sunflower oil
125 ml (4 fl oz) water
½ tsp flaked tuna
5 g (⅛ oz) dried pasta
½ tsp freshly chopped flat-leaf parsley

Cut all the fish into small cubes. Cut the prawns into small pieces. Finely dice
the courgette.

Heat the oil in a saucepan and sauté the diced courgette. Add the water, the
flaked tuna and the pasta. Bring to the boil and simmer for 10 minutes.

Add the fish cubes and prawns to the soup and simmer on a low heat for
10 minutes until cooked through. Remove the soup from the heat and allow to
cool. Stir in the parsley. Serve a portion at a time.

Beef pot for Tiger

Makes 2 to 3 portions

100 g (3½ oz) beef
1 tsp sunflower oil
125 ml (4 fl oz) water
10 g (¼ oz) potato
10 g (¼ oz) French beans
¼ tsp additive-free vegetable stock powder
½ tsp freshly chopped flat-leaf parsley

Cut the beef into very small pieces. Heat the sunflower oil in a saucepan
and brown the meat. Add the water and cook, covered, for 20 minutes.

Meanwhile, peel and finely grate the potato. Wash and trim the beans, and
chop them finely. Add the grated potato, beans and stock powder to the meat.
Simmer these together for a further 15 minutes.

Remove from the heat and allow to cool. Stir in the chopped parsley.
Serve a portion at a time.

LIVER DUMPLING SOUP

Makes 2 to 3 portions

1 egg yolk
10 g (¼ oz) instant porridge oats
70 g (2½ oz) fresh beef mince
30 g (1 oz) beef liver, puréed
½ tsp freshly chopped flat-leaf parsley
5 g (⅛ oz) carrot, peeled
5 g (⅛ oz) celery stick
250 ml (8 fl oz) water
¼ tsp additive-free vegetable stock powder

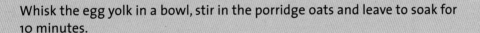

Whisk the egg yolk in a bowl, stir in the porridge oats and leave to soak for 10 minutes.

Add the beef mince, puréed beef liver and parsley. Knead these together. With damp hands, shape the beef mixture into small balls.

Finely grate the carrot and celery. Put the water in a saucepan with the vegetables and stock powder, and bring to the boil. Add the meatballs and cook for 10 minutes on a low heat.

Remove the soup from the heat and allow to cool. Serve a portion at a time of the liver dumplings, along with a little of the liquid.

HEARTY MEALS

TURKEY STRIPS

Makes 2 to 3 portions

100 g (3½ oz) turkey breast, skinless
1 tsp sesame oil
2 tbsp water
10 g (¼ oz) cooked rice
1 tbsp cream
10 g (¼ oz) alfalfa sprouts, finely chopped
½ tsp desiccated coconut

Cut the turkey breast into thin strips. Heat the sesame oil in a saucepan, sauté the turkey breast strips, add 2 tablespoons of water and cook for 10 minutes.

Remove the pan from the heat and allow to cool. Mix in the rice, cream, alfalfa sprouts and desiccated coconut. Serve a portion at a time.

SALLY'S FAVOURITE FISH

Makes 2 to 3 portions

100 g (3½ oz) salmon fillet, skinned and boned
1 tsp olive oil
2 tbsp water
15 g (½ oz) spinach, finely chopped
10 g (¼ oz) chopped cooked noodles
1 tbsp crème fraîche

Cut the salmon into very small cubes. Heat the oil in a saucepan
and sauté the salmon. Add 2 tablespoons of water, the spinach
and the noodles. Cook for 10 minutes.

Remove the pan from the heat and allow to cool.
Gently stir in the crème fraîche. Serve a portion at a time.

LADY'S CHEESE BALLS

Makes 2 to 3 portions

1 egg yolk
1 tbsp instant porridge oats
15 g (½ oz) peeled, cooked pumpkin
80 g (2¾ oz) fresh beef mince
½ tsp freshly chopped flat-leaf parsley
20 g (¾ oz) mozzarella cheese
1 tsp vegetable oil

Whisk the egg yolk in a bowl, stir in the porridge oats and leave to soak for 10 minutes.

Finely dice the pumpkin. Add it to the porridge oats and egg mixture, together with the beef mince and parsley, and knead.

Cut the mozzarella into 3 slices and shape the meat mixture into 6 meatballs. Sandwich each slice of mozzarella between two meatballs and flatten down slightly.

Heat the oil in a frying pan and fry the meatballs on a medium heat for 3 minutes on each side.

Remove from the pan and leave to cool. Serve a portion at a time, cut into manageable-sized pieces.

CASSEROLE WITH HEART

Makes 2 to 3 portions

70 g (2½ oz) chicken breast fillet, skinless
30 g (1 oz) chicken hearts
150 ml (5 fl oz) water
1 tsp butter
1 tsp plain flour
1 tbsp cream
1 tbsp grated cheese
15 g (½ oz) Little Gem lettuce
10 g (¼ oz) cooked rice

Put the chicken breast fillet and chicken hearts in a saucepan with the water. Bring to the boil and cook for 15 minutes. Drain the meat, reserving the cooking liquid. Allow the meat to cool, and cut into small pieces.

Melt the butter in a small saucepan, stir in the flour and cook for a short time. Add 4 tablespoons of the cooking liquid plus the cream, and bring to the boil. Stir in the cheese so that it melts into the sauce. Remove the saucepan from the heat and allow to cool.

Wash the Little Gem lettuce and finely chop. Mix the rice, meat and lettuce with the sauce. Serve a portion at a time.

LEROY'S LIVER STEW

Makes 2 to 3 portions

100 g (3½ oz) beef liver
1 tsp sunflower oil
3 tbsp water
15 g (½ oz) peeled, cooked potato
1 tbsp crème fraîche
1 tsp freshly chopped flat-leaf parsley

Wash the beef liver, pat it dry and cut it into small cubes. Heat the oil in a saucepan and add the cubes of liver. Allow the liver to brown, then add the water and cook for 10 minutes on a medium heat.

Mash the potato with a fork, then mix it into the liver stew, together with the crème fraîche and parsley. Allow to cool. Serve a portion at a time.

PAULA'S STIR-FRIED FISH

Makes 2 to 3 portions

100 g (3½ oz) mackerel fillet, skinned and boned
10 g (¾ oz) courgette
1 tsp olive oil
2 tsp tomato purée
2 tbsp water
10 g (¼ oz) cooked rice
2 tsp cream
½ tsp freshly chopped basil

Cut the mackerel fillet into small cubes. Finely grate the courgette.

Heat the oil in a frying pan and stir-fry the fish and courgette over a medium heat.
Add the tomato purée, the water and the rice to the pan. Simmer for 10 minutes.

Remove from the heat and allow to cool. Mix in the cream and the basil.
Serve a portion at a time.

Lamb hotpot with carrot

Makes 2 to 3 portions

100 g (3½ oz) lamb
20 g (¾ oz) carrot
1 tsp olive oil
2 tbsp water
1 tbsp natural yogurt
½ tsp freshly chopped flat-leaf parsley

Cut the lamb into small cubes. Peel and finely grate the carrot.

Heat the olive oil in a frying pan and brown the meat on all sides.
Add the grated carrot, followed by the water. Cook on a medium heat for
10 minutes. Remove from the heat and allow to cool.

Mix in the yogurt and the parsley. Serve a portion at a time.

ITALIAN
FOR TIGERS

VITELLO TONNATO

Makes 2 to 3 portions

60 g (2 oz) veal cutlet
1 tsp olive oil
2 tbsp water
1 anchovy fillet in oil
40 g (1½ oz) tinned tuna in brine, drained
2 tbsp natural yogurt
½ tsp freshly chopped basil

Pound the veal cutlet until very thin. Heat the oil in a frying pan and fry the meat for 1 minute on each side. Remove it from the pan, allow to cool and cut into small pieces.

Loosen the pan residues with the water and allow to cool. Rinse off the anchovy fillet, pat it dry, place it in a blender together with the tuna, yogurt and pan residues. Purée, then mix the basil into the sauce.

Serve the pieces of meat with the tuna sauce, a portion at a time.

CARPACCIO CARUSO

Makes 1 portion

40 g (1½ oz) very fresh raw beef
5 g (⅛ oz) mixed salad leaves (e.g. rocket, Little Gem lettuce)
½ tsp olive oil
1 tbsp water
¼ tsp grated Parmesan cheese

Cut the meat into very thin strips, flatten them slightly with the back of a knife and arrange on a plate.

Finely chop the salad leaves. In a bowl, mix the olive oil with the water to make a dressing, and mix with the chopped salad leaves.

Sprinkle it over the meat and scatter the Parmesan on top. Serve immediately.

Tip
Many cats see raw meat as prey that first has to be captured and killed. As such, to avoid a lot of mess around the house, the carpaccio should be served outside. Alternatively, fresh beef mince can be used, mixed with the salad leaves and the Parmesan cheese.

BOLOGNESE À LA NERO

Makes 2 to 3 portions

10 g (¼ oz) carrot, peeled
5 g (⅛ oz) celery stick
1 tsp olive oil
100 g (3½ oz) fresh beef mince
2 tsp tomato purée
4 tbsp water
10 g (¼ oz) chopped cooked pasta
1 tsp grated Parmesan

Grate the carrot and finely chop the celery.

Heat the olive oil in a saucepan and fry the beef mince until crumbly.
Add the vegetables and tomato purée, and cook for a short time.
Pour in the water and cook for a further 10 minutes.

Mix the Bolognese sauce with the pasta and allow to cool.
Scatter the Parmesan on top, and serve a portion at a time.

LUCCA'S FAVOURITE RISOTTO

Makes 2 to 3 portions

100 g (3½ oz) chicken breast fillet, skinless
15 g (½ oz) green asparagus
1 tsp olive oil
10 g (¼ oz) arborio rice
5 tbsp home-made chicken stock, see p. 8 (alternatively, dissolve ¼ tsp
  additive-free vegetable stock powder in 5 tbsp water)
¼ tsp butter
1 tsp grated Parmesan cheese

Cut the chicken breast fillet into small cubes. Finely chop the asparagus.

Heat the olive oil in a saucepan and sauté the cubes of meat. Add the rice and
asparagus, and sauté briefly. Add 2 tablespoons of the stock and continue
stirring until the liquid has almost evaporated. Add the rest of the stock and
cook uncovered on a low heat for 15 minutes, stirring occasionally

Remove the risotto from the heat, stir in the butter and Parmesan cheese, and
allow to cool. Serve a portion at a time.

FRITTATA FOR MIDGE

Makes 2 to 3 portions

50 g (1¾ oz) cooked peeled prawns (without preservatives)
1 egg
2 tbsp low fat cream cheese
½ tsp grated Parmesan cheese
5 g (⅛ oz) porridge oats
15 g (½ oz) spinach, finely chopped
1 tsp olive oil

Cut the prawns into small pieces. Mix the egg, cream cheese and Parmesan cheese in a bowl. Stir the porridge oats, prawns and spinach into the egg mixture.

Heat the olive oil in a small frying pan, add the egg mixture and cook on a medium heat for 8 minutes. Turn and cook for a further 2 minutes.

Remove the frittata from the pan, allow to cool and cut into small pieces. Serve a portion at a time.

THE CAT'S WHISKERS – FINE DINING FOR YOUR CAT

LULU'S CHICKEN AND TUNA SALAD

Makes 2 to 3 portions

50 g (1¾ oz) tinned tuna (in brine)
50 g (1¾ oz) cooked chicken
15 g (½ oz) mixed salad leaves (e.g. radicchio, looseleaf lettuce,
  Little Gem lettuce)
5 g (⅛ oz) beetroot
1 tsp vegetable oil
1 tbsp natural yogurt
1 tbsp water
½ tsp freshly chopped flat-leaf parsley

Drain and flake the tuna. Cut the chicken into small pieces. Wash the salad leaves, shake them dry and cut into very thin strips. Chop the beetroot. Place all the prepared ingredients into a bowl and mix.

In a small bowl, whisk the oil and yogurt with the water to make a dressing, then stir in the parsley.

Serve the meat and vegetable mixture a portion at a time, with some of the dressing drizzled on top.

RABBIT STEW

Makes 2 to 3 portions

100 g (3½ oz) rabbit
1 tsp olive oil
10 g (¼ oz) potato
10 g (¼ oz) chicory
3 tbsp home-made chicken stock, see p. 8 (alternatively, dissolve ¼ tsp
  of additive-free vegetable stock powder in 3 tbsp water)
¼ tsp chopped hazelnuts
½ tsp freshly chopped flat-leaf parsley

Cut the rabbit into small cubes. Heat the oil in a saucepan and brown the cubes of meat.

Peel and grate the potato, cut the chicory into thin strips and add both to the meat in the saucepan. Add the stock and cook covered for 10 minutes.

Remove the stew from the heat and allow to cool. Mix in the hazelnuts and parsley. Serve a portion at a time.

'MIAOW' PRAWN COCKTAIL

Makes 2 to 3 portions

75 g (2½ oz) cooked peeled prawns (without preservatives)
2 tbsp natural yogurt
1 tsp tomato purée
1 tsp vegetable oil
10 g (¼ oz) alfalfa sprouts
½ tsp freshly chopped flat-leaf parsley

Cut the prawns into small pieces. Mix the yogurt, tomato purée and vegetable oil together to make a sauce. Chop the alfalfa sprouts.

Mix the prawns, sprouts and parsley with the sauce. Serve a portion at a time.

POULTRY NUGGETS IN ASPIC

Fills three 100 ml (3½ fl oz) moulds

50 g (1¾ oz) chicken
50 g (1¾ oz) duck
1 tsp sesame oil
200 ml (7 fl oz) home-made chicken stock, see p. 8
  (alternatively, dissolve ½ tsp of additive-free vegetable
  stock powder in 200 ml/7 fl oz of water)
15 g (½ oz) iceberg lettuce
10 g (¼ oz) cooked rice
1 tsp of granulated gelatine

Cut the chicken and duck into small cubes.

Heat the oil in a saucepan and sauté the meat. Pour in the stock and cook
for 10 minutes.

Meanwhile, cut the iceberg lettuce into thin strips. Remove the meat from
the stock and mix with the lettuce and rice. Divide the mixture between
the 3 moulds (for example, empty foil catfood cartons). Add the gelatine to
the stock in the saucepan and stir vigorously until it is dissolved. Fill up the
moulds and place them in the refrigerator for 3 hours.

To serve one portion, loosen the edges with a knife. Dip the mould briefly into
hot water and turn it out. Allow to stand at room temperature for 30 minutes
before serving.

SALMON TROUT MOUSSE FOR LUCKY

Fills two 75 ml (2½ fl oz) moulds

15 g (½ oz) courgette
80 g (3 oz) salmon trout fillet
1 tsp sunflower oil
4 tbsp water
⅔ tsp of granulated gelatine
1 tbsp low fat cream cheese
1 tbsp double cream

Grate the courgette, and cut the salmon trout fillet into small cubes.

Heat the oil in a saucepan and sauté the cubes of fish. Add the water and cook for 5 minutes. Remove from the heat, place in a high-sided container and purée with a hand-held blender.

Add the gelatine and stir it into the purée so that it dissolves. Make sure the purée is very hot or it won't dissolve. Fold in the courgette, cream cheese and double cream. Divide the mixture between the moulds and place in the refrigerator for 3 hours.

To serve a portion, remove a mould from the refrigerator and carefully loosen the edges with a knife. Dip the moulds briefly into hot water and turn the mousse out. Allow to stand at room temperature for 30 minutes.

KITTY TREATS

FISH MUNCHIES AND CHICKEN CHIPS

Makes 2 to 3 portions

150 g (5½ oz) chicken breast fillet, skinless
150 g (5½ oz) mackerel fillet, skinless and boneless

Preheat the oven to 150°C/300°F/Gas Mark 2, and line two baking
trays with baking paper. Cut the chicken breast into wafer-thin slices.
Carefully pound each slice flat between sheets of clingfilm, and lay the
slices on one of the baking trays.

Cut the mackerel fillet first into 5 mm (¼-inch) thick slices, then into 1 cm x 1 cm
(½-inch x ½-inch) squares. Spread out the fish pieces on the second baking tray.

Put the two baking trays in the preheated oven for 25 minutes. Reduce the
temperature to 100°C/200°F/Gas Mark ¼, open the oven door a crack and allow the
snacks to dry for a further 40 minutes.

Turn off the oven, and leave the fish munchies and chicken chips to dry out overnight.
You can store them in an airtight container in a cool, dry place for a fortnight.
Make sure that they are completely cool and dried out and that they do not contain
any residual moisture.

LIVER PIE

Makes two pies

50 g (1¾ oz) flour
10 g (¼ oz) butter
3 tbsp cold water
100 g (3½ oz) beef liver
100 g (3½ oz) fresh beef
  mince

1 egg yolk
½ tsp freshly chopped flat-leaf parsley
butter for greasing
flour for dusting
1 tbsp cream

Knead the flour, butter and water together to make a dough, wrap in clingfilm and leave to rest in the refrigerator for 30 minutes.

Wash the beef liver, pat it dry and cut it into very small pieces. Place in a bowl and mix with the beef mince, egg yolk and parsley.

Preheat the oven to 180°C/350°F/Gas Mark 4. Grease two small tartlet cases or bun tins and dust with flour. Roll out the pastry very thinly to make two circles, and use these to line the moulds. Cut off any protruding edges and fill with the meat mixture.

With the leftover pastry, roll out two circles the same size as the moulds and cut a hole in the centre of each. Put the pastry lids onto the pies and press the edges together. Brush the pies with the cream, and bake in the preheated oven for approximately 30–40 minutes.

Remove from the oven and allow to cool. You can feed your cat little chunks of pie as a reward.

Tip
The pies keep for a maximum of 2 days in the refrigerator. It is therefore advisable to freeze the second pie immediately.

POULTRY HEARTS

Makes 2 to 3 portions

100 g (3½ oz) plain flour, plus extra for dusting
20 g (¾ oz) oat bran
2 tsp grated Parmesan cheese
1 egg yolk
10 g (¼ oz) butter
100 g (3½ oz) cooked poultry, puréed
  (e.g. jar of turkey-based baby food)

For glazing:
1 egg yolk
1 tbsp single cream

Knead the first six ingredients into a smooth dough. Wrap the dough in clingfilm
and leave to rest for one hour in the refrigerator.

Preheat the oven to 180°C/350°F/Gas Mark 4. Remove the dough from the refrigerator
and roll it out to about 3 mm (⅛ inch) thick on a floured work surface. Cut out small
heart shapes with a cutter.

Line a baking tray with baking paper and lay the hearts on top. Whisk together the egg
yolk and cream in a small bowl, and brush the hearts with this mixture.
Bake in the preheated oven for 15 minutes.

Turn off the oven, open the door a crack and leave the poultry hearts in the oven to
harden. You can store the biscuits in an airtight container in a cool, dry place for
a fortnight. Make sure that they are completely cool and dried out and that they do
not contain any residual moisture.

Picture acknowledgements
Corbis: 16 Don Mason
Getty Images: 1 Imagemore, 6 Peter Cade,
32 Brian Gordon Green, 44 GK Hart/
Vikki Hart, 56 Sharon Dominick